Landscape History

Clive H. Knowles

The British landscape is the product of
centuries of human activity. Each
generation has left its mark, adding new
features of its own, and modifying or
erasing those it has inherited from the past.
The task of the landscape historian is to
disentangle the different elements in this
intricate, ever-changing pattern, and to
establish when, how and why each came to
be added - or removed. This pamphlet
examines the value and interest of
landscape history, using examples drawn
from different periods and regions.

The Historical Association aims to develop
public interest in history and to advance its
study and teaching at all levels.
Membership is open to everyone. Further
information is available from The
Secretary, The Historical Association, 59a
Kennington Park Road, London SE11 4JH.

GENERAL SERIES 107

Landscape History

CLIVE H. KNOWLES

493920

The Historical Association
59a Kennington Park Road, London SE11 4JH

ACKNOWLEDGEMENTS

Outside front cover: Braunston, Northamptonshire, reproduced by courtesy of Cambridge University Collection (Crown Copyright Reserved); *Figure 1:* Cambridge University Collection, (Crown Copyright Reserved); *Figure 2:* Map reproduced by courtesy of Professor J.K.S. St Joseph, photograph reproduced by courtesy of Cambridge University Collection, (Crown Copyright Reserved); *Figure 3:* Reproduced by courtesy of Cambridge University Collection; *Figure 4:* Reproduced by courtesy of Aerofilms Ltd; *Figure 5:* Reproduced by courtesy of Cambridge University Collection; *Figure 6:* Reproduced by courtesy of Aerofilms Ltd; *Figure 7:* Photograph reproduced by courtesy of Aerofilms, line drawings reproduced by courtesy of Professor M.W. Beresford; *Figure 8:* Reproduced by courtesy of Hodder & Stoughton, from J.M. Steane, *The Northamptonshire Landscape* (1974, figure 17). *Figure 9:* Kip's engraving reproduced by courtesy of the Marquess of Bath, Longleat House, Warminster, Wiltshire; *Figure 10:* photograph reproduced by courtesy of Aerofilms Ltd; *Figure 11:* Photograph 'Satanic Mills' taken by Randolf Lagenbach, and reproduced in *Country Life* 8 February, 1979.

©Clive H. Knowles

ISBN 085278 263 2

HA 8.5/7/83

Originated and published by
The Historical Association

Printed in Great Britain by The Chameleon Press Limited, 5-25 Burr Road, Wandsworth, London SW18 4SG

Contents

Figure 1: *Barton Broad, Norfolk, looking north: the peninuslas and lines of reed-swamp, which mark the position of balks of peat between diggings, run at slightly different angles on either side of the former Barton-Irstead parish boundary.*

The Nature of Landscape History

Landscape history is a new and fascinating branch of historical study.[1] Its main threads were first drawn together in Professor W.G. Hoskins's *The Making of the English Landscape,* published as recently as 1955. By the searching questions it asked and the range of material it employed, that deservedly famous book profoundly altered our understanding of our surroundings and produced, in the words of one reviewer, 'a permanent and delightful enlargement of consciousness'.

The most influential traditions in British topographical writing had hitherto been the antiquarian and the sentimental. The antiquarian was easily the older form. Writers such as John Leland in the 1540s, John Aubrey a century later, and William Stukeley in the early eighteenth century, minutely described countless buildings, earthworks and stone circles. Their books and papers remain invaluable sources of information about often vanished features, but they made only fitful attempts to establish the historical meaning and the original settings of the monuments they so laboriously recorded.[2]

The other mode of topographical writing was strongly sentimental, and permeated with nostalgia for an older, vanishing Britain. In the 1930s, for example, Charles Bradley Ford's *The Landscape of England* (1933), Sir William Beach-Thomas's *The English Landscape* (1938), and the volumes of the 'County Landscapes' series, sought to evoke the beauty of unspoilt countryside and showpiece villages and towns; urban, industrial Britain was a disfigurement to be deplored and largely ignored. What is more, though their leisurely descriptions were lovingly observed, their historical explanations of the appearance of the landscape were unsystematic and superficial.

For W.G. Hoskins, much of this popular writing was 'sentimental and formless slush'. The approach he advocated was analytical, scholarly and far more probing.[3]

He compared the landscape to a symphony which though it can be enjoyed as 'an architectural mass of sound' is much more interesting and meaningful if 'we are able to isolate the themes as they enter, to see how one by one they are intricately woven together and by what magic new harmonies are produced'.[4] Though archaeologists like O.G.S. Crawford and historical geographers such as H.C. Darby had already been writing good landscape history,[5] Hoskins had the distinction of producing the first book to explore the historical evolution of the English landscape, and to analyse the forces which have shaped its changing face. The importance of his achievement was not immediately recognised, especially by the scholarly world. It is curious to recall now that *The Economic History Review* ignored the book and *The English Historical Review* favoured it only with a 'short notice'. As Hoskins himself wryly observed 'I ought to have called it *The Morphogenesis of the Cultural Environment* to make the fullest impact'.[6] More than a decade elapsed before it was fully acknowledged as opening a new era in landscape studies, and the trickle of works on landscape history became a spate. Two successful BBC TV series on the landscape prepared by Hoskins, who also wrote the booklets to accompany them,[7] further fuelled a growing public interest which led in 1979 to the setting up of a separate 'Society for Landscape Studies' with its own journal, *Landscape History*.

Scope

The contrast in tone and content between books on the landscape written before 1955 and those published in increasing numbers afterwards is an index of the eventual impact of Hoskins's book. Most, but by no means all, of the sentimentalism has gone. In its place is a much more precise understanding of what landscape is, and a far more searching investigation of the historical processes which have moulded it through the ages. Landscape is now defined as the product of man's manipulation of the physical environment. As such it is an expression of his economic activities, his social relationships, his artistic aspirations, his religious persuasions, and even his recreations. All of society's attitudes and priorities are displayed in the landscape.

Such an interpretation has many implications. One is that landscape is an intensely localised thing which differs from area to area according to the underlying geology and physical features as well as man's varying impact on them. In the judgement of some writers, it is reasonable to speak not of one but of many landscapes, even in an area as small as an English county. Whether it is possible in Britain to distinguish readily between landscape and scenery is a more controversial matter. In his television series 'One Man's England', as the helicopter swept in over the magnificent coastline of Cornwall, Hoskins commented 'this is *scenery* rather than landscape. In fact it is rather like looking at a pretty woman who has no intelligence. I expect a landscape to speak to me and to ask questions – or rather pose problems, which merely pretty scenery does not'.[8] Such a view seems to underestimate the extent of man's influence on his surroundings. As long ago as the eighteenth century one writer was able to assert that 'no spot on this island can be said to be in a state of Nature. There is not a tree, perhaps not a bush, now standing upon the face of the country which owes its identical state to Nature alone'.[9] There may be some parts of Britain unaffected by man, but as often as Hoskins has pointed to an example of untouched natural scenery, other experts have disproved his claim.[10]

But the most important implication is that landscape, by its very nature, is not the unchanging background to man's activities. On the contrary, if differs from period to period as well as from area to area. Each generation has left its mark on the landscape, adding new features of its own, and modifying or erasing those it has inherited from the past. The aim of the landscape historian, therefore, is to disentangle the different elements in this intricate, ever-changing pattern, and to establish how, why and when each came to be added – or removed.

Materials

Documents, maps, pictures, and the landscape itself figure amongst the vast range of sources which can be made to yield clues to the appearance of past landscapes. Their various uses can only be touched on here. Almost any document can be used for landscape history, but two

categories are especially important for the kinds of landscape evidence they provide. By far the larger is composed
of those records which give us information about the
spatial distribution of man's impact on his surroundings.
For England, the earliest and best known is Domesday
Book, an invaluable guide to its population and resources
in the eleventh century, though its limitations are increasingly evident. Poll taxes, lay subsidies, tithe surveys
and enclosure records are just a few of the sources which
provide a wealth of material for later centuries.[11] Wales, on
the other hand, has a paucity of early sources, and the first
comprehensive written record for Scotland is the First
Statistical Account, published in the 1790s.

Descriptive accounts make up the other main category of
documentary evidence. Though they may have lacked
something in historical curiosity, travel writers like Celia
Fiennes in the seventeenth century and Daniel Defoe in the
eighteenth, are especially important for their firsthand
accounts of the landscapes they saw on their tours.

Maps and plans provide a visual key to landscape change
and a framework for understanding evidence derived from
other sources. In England, estate and town maps begin in
the sixteenth century, and many counties were mapped in
detail in the eighteenth, though the results vary in quality
and cannot be taken at face value. The first comprehensive
maps of Scotland are William Roy's military surveys
(1747-55), and of Wales, the surveyors' drawings (1809-20)
which formed the basis of the Ordnance Survey's first
one-inch maps. Other, larger scale Ordnance Survey maps
were provided for the whole country in the course of the
nineteenth century. All these maps present their material in
an accurate and uniform way, but it must always be
remembered that they were surveyed and reprinted over
long periods.[12] Maps, too, are invaluable for place-name
studies which, by tracing the derivation of certain topographical names, can sometimes throw light on the appearance of the landscape when they were first used.[13] Topographical prints and pictures often provide arresting
glimpses of past landscapes. Amongst the best are the
bird's eye views or aerial surveys popular in the seventeenth and eighteenth centuries, which enable us to trace
the development of many country houses and parks.[14]

Finally, there is the landscape itself which, as Hoskins has always insisted, 'to those who know how to read it aright, is the richest historical record we possess'. This is because it contains vestiges of earlier landscapes which can be used to confirm conclusions drawn from documentary sources, or as the starting point for fresh explorations in landscape history. It can be exploited in many different ways. Aerial photography, for instance, can bring out the relationship of features better than any map, as well as revealing crop marks and undulations in the ground which are clues to remains lying beneath the surface. Archaeology, in its turn, has contributed immeasurably to the study of landscape history, not simply by providing evidence of the changing nature and distribution of human habitations, but by enabling the plant ecologist, using carbon dating techniques, to establish the approximate dates of early vegetational and land use changes. But most important of all is the exploration of the ground on foot, because everything in the present-day landscape can reveal something about the past if we know how to interpret it. Recent discoveries about hedgerows serve to illustrate this. Botanical surveys suggest that the number of species in a hedge is an indication of its age, the more shrubs it contains the older it is.[15] The use of this technique is already making possible discoveries 'for which no written documents exist, or have ever existed'.[16]

Method

The first concern of the landscape historian is to identify patterns, because it is these which give distinctive character to an area. Geometrically shaped fields, for example, may indicate an agricultural landscape planned by eighteenth- or early nineteenth-century parliamentary enclosure commissioners. But individual features will also attract his attention, especially if they appear anomalous. An isolated church with no settlement nearby may often, but by no means always, signify that a village has shifted or even disappeared; a tight curve in a railway line may prove to be a visible reminder of a landowner's refusal to allow the railway to cross his landscaped park.[17] The landscape historian can employ these materials and methods in many fruitful ways. He can, for example, examine the origins and significance of selected man-made features in today's landscape which we owe to earlier times. Or he can try to reconstruct some past landscape, in part or in its entirety, and explore the processes which brought it into being or caused it to disappear.

Landscape history is a difficult and demanding subject, full of pitfalls for the unwary. In the sections which follow, different examples have been chosen to illustrate its interest and value and to suggest the endless discoveries still waiting to be made.

Present Landscapes

The man-made landscape we have inherited from earlier times can produce a variety of reactions. To some, it is an incomprehensible jumble of objects 'messy and disorganized, like a book with pages missing, torn, and smudged; a book whose copy has been edited and re-edited by people with illegible handwriting'.[18] To others, historic houses and picturesque villages have instant appeal, but the rest of the landscape, especially recent changes in it, may be dismissed as uninteresting, or simply ignored.

The immediate fascination of landscape history is that it can make our surroundings, however familiar and apparently commonplace, much more interesting and enjoyable. By enabling us to disentangle each element in the pattern, and to study the processes which brought it into being, it makes it possible, in Hoskins's words, 'to look at every feature with exact knowledge, able to give a name to it and knowing how it got there, and not just to gaze uncomprehendingly at it...'.[19]

The Making of the Broads

The Norfolk Broads are enjoyed by thousands of holiday-makers every year, yet down to the 1950s the origin of these beautiful inland waters was still a mystery. Their sheer size - in the late nineteenth century, before more recent encroachment by vegetation, they covered 2,600 acres to an average depth of 8 feet - and their irregular shape, seemed to rule out the possibility that they were man-made (**Figure 1**). Admittedly, there was no evidence they existed before the early fourteenth century, but it was generally assumed that they were natural features, the result of marine flooding, possibly as far back as Roman times. It required the collaboration of a geomorphologist, a botanist, an engineer, an archaeologist, and a historical geographer, to demonstrate that the Broads were the unwitting creation of medieval peat-diggers. In those times, Norfolk was a thickly populated area with a

11

well-developed salt-making industry. Woodland was scarce, but there was an abundance of peat, and the account rolls of the great monastic houses reveal a vast trade in turves from the thirteenth to the fifteenth centuries. The manor of South Walsham belonging to St Benet's Abbey alone produced 250,000 turves a year in 1260s, and the fires of Norwich Cathedral Priory consumed over 400,000 in a single year early in the fourteenth century.

Once it was realised that the present-day Broads were the only area from which such huge quantities of peat could have come, close study of their steep sides and horizontal floors confirmed that they were created in the course of peat extraction. The basins became flooded, it was concluded, when the land sank several feet in relation to sea-level in the later Middle Ages. The strings of islets of uncut peat which are such a distinctive feature of some of the Broads were now identified as sections preserved from digging because they were parish boundaries, access routes, or the limits of different turbaries, a number of which, employing dredging methods, remained in use long after the peat was under water. So it is to the extraction of 900 million cubic feet of peat by long-forgotten generations of peat-diggers that we owe the most extraordinary landscape modification of medieval times.[20]

The English Village

The traditional English village, clustered around its parish church and green, or strung out along its main street, is generally seen as one of the most stable and enduring features of the landscape. Such villages are commonly thought to have been founded by the invading Anglo-Saxons and mentioned in Domesday Book, and throughout all the vicissitudes of their history to have occupied the same site and maintained their present form. So convinced were some geographers that our villages had changed little in a thousand years, that they constructed elaborate classifications of layout based on modern evidence. In fact, the modern face of the English village hides a many-layered story whose theme is change rather than stability.

Evidence is rapidly accumulating that the Anglo-Saxons lived, not in nucleated villages, but in scattered farmsteads and hamlets, many of short duration. The way entries in

Domesday Book are arranged according to land-ownership rather than settlements may conceal a similar situation in the late eleventh century. Even where continuity of name can be demonstrated, it is clear that villages moved their sites and often radically altered their layouts in medieval and later times.[21] At East Witton in Wensleydale, North Yorkshire, the layout of houses clustered around a green with a church at its head suggests the timeless pattern of the English village (**Figure 2**). So it is disconcerting to find, on closer examination, that the church was built by the Earl of Ailesbury in 1809 to mark George III's jubilee, and that the houses surrounding the green are of the same date. If this leads us to conclude that East Witton is no more than an early nineteenth-century estate village bearing witness to the philanthropy of a local landowner, that too proves to be mistaken. A map made in 1627 by William Senior 'Professor of Arithmetique, Geometrie, Astronomie, Navigation and Dialling, well-wisher to the Mathematiques' reveals that the nineteenth-century village was simply a rebuilding of an earlier settlement standing on precisely the same site. It also shows that East Witton's original church and its accompanying straggle of houses lay south-east of the present village (**Figure 2**). Other evidence suggests that this settlement was superseded nearly seven hundred years ago when Jervaulx Abbey, the largest local landowner of the time, laid out the 'green' village as the site of a new market first held in 1307.[22] Elsewhere, such as Norfolk, field-walking and excavation have revealed that many villages moved their sites as many as three times before the fifteenth century. What makes East Witton unusual is that we can make an informed guess as to when and why its migration took place.

One reason why house sites were so fluid and settlements could migrate so easily was that, down to early modern times, most cottages and houses were flimsy structures which, as excavation of deserted sites has shown, needed to be rebuilt every generation or so. This conclusion points to another common misconception about the appearance of the English village; that its picturesque old houses were the former homes of medieval peasants. These 'olde worlde' cottages generally turn out to have belonged to the well-off yeomen and husbandmen and frequently date from the years between 1570 and 1640. During this prosperous and

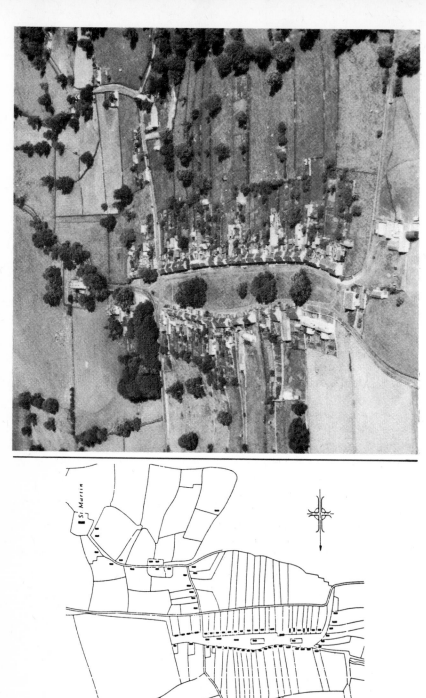

Figure 2: *East Witton, Yorkshire: left in 1627, redrawn after the plan by William Senior; right, in 1953, looking east.*

expansive period, Professor Hoskins contended, there was a wave of building and modernization, fuelled by greater wealth and a desire for improved comfort, which he called the 'Great Rebuilding of Rural England'. But whether we think in terms of a well-defined housing revolution or, as others have argued, successive rebuildings from the sixteenth century onwards, it is clear that the rich variety of English regional building styles – from 'black and white' to Cotswold stone – is the achievement of the two centuries between 1570 and 1770.[23]

As some English villages flourished and were rebuilt in more permanent form, others withered or disappeared altogether. At Great Stretton in Leicestershire, for instance, a village of fifteen households in 1563 had been reduced to a handful of families in 1670, shortly after the enclosure of its open fields.[24] Today the site of the village is indicated only by an isolated church (rebuilt in 1838), the moated enclosure of the manor house, and the remains of house plots and holloways or deeply-worn former streets, the whole surrounded by the corrugated pattern of ridge-and-furrow created by ploughing in the years before desertion (**Figure 3**). The ravages of the Black Death, the clearances for sheep farming in the fifteenth, and the demands of landscape gardening in the eighteenth century, all contributed to the toll of villages. But it is important to realise that villages disappeared all the time – indeed still do. Desertion is a normal part of settlement history. Now that over 3,000 sites are known, the deserted village site must take its place alongside the village itself as one of the characteristic features of our landscape.[25]

The Meaning of High-Rise Housing

Compared to landscapes of the historic depth of English villages, blocks of high-rise flats in our cities may seem unpromising material for the landscape historian. Even in the 1960s, the peak period of multi-storey housing, they never represented more than 20 per cent of total local authority housing, and surely they are too recent to be of much interest. Yet the visual importance of these towers, singly or in groups, in cities such as London, Birmingham and Sheffield, has been enormous, radically changing their skylines. They represent, moreover, a complete departure from

Figure 3: *Great Stretton, Leicestershire: the site of the deserted village.*

the traditional English urban landscape of low terraces and semi-detached houses.[26] The rise and fall of this un-English form of housing not only throws into relief some important social questions but represents a crucial chapter in modern landscape history.

'The suburb', declared the 1933 International Congress of Modern Architecture, 'is the symbol of waste...a kind of scum churning against the walls of the city...one of the greatest evils of the century.' As it swallowed up the countryside, replacing it with miles of repetitive, semi-detached houses, spreading suburbia caused consternation amongst pioneer conservationists before the Second World War and provoked John Betjeman into writing a poem in 1937 which pointed to the one advantage a war would bring:

'Come, friendly bombs, and fall on Slough
It isn't fit for humans now.'[27]

Architects and planners, for their part, were increasingly inspired by Le Corbusier's vision of 'cities in the air', flatted towers set in open spaces, which would prevent further sprawl by accommodating city dwellers within the existing built-up areas.

In the great post-war reconstruction, local authorities set out to transform the face of British cities. Sheffield was one of the earliest to embrace a high-rise policy. In 1955 a deputation returned from a tour of Continental flatted estates to advise the council that 'in the circumstances now obtaining in Sheffield - land shortage, ever increasing distances between houses and work-places, immobility of heavy industry and the urgency of slum clearance - the deputation is convinced of the need to introduce schemes of multi-storey flats...'. Park Hill, with its remarkable street decks, and other more conventional high blocks were soon transforming the city's appearance (**Figure 4**). Everywhere the tide flowed strongly in favour of high-rise housing. Governments of both persuasions provided financial incentives, after 1956 even paying larger subsidies the higher the blocks. Drawing on Continental experience, industrialised building methods using precast concrete blocks were developed to make construction easier if not cheaper. There was even an unspoken argument of political advantage in favour of high-rise housing: Labour urban councils could thereby

Figure 4: *Sheffield: Norfolk Park development, built in the 1960s.*

retain working-class supporters and Conservative rural councils no longer needed to fear an influx of workers undermining their electoral control.

Disillusionment came swiftly. By the mid-sixties, local authorities were finding increasing difficulty in letting their high-rise flats. Government ministers might inveigh against 'this foolish prejudice against flats', but for those expected to live in these barrack-like towers devoid of community feeling, the planners dream had turned into a nightmare. The pressure for a return to human-scale housing grew. Then, in 1968, an explosion in a kitchen on the eighteenth floor of Ronan Point in the London borough of Newham, bringing loss of life and the partial collapse of the building, completed public disenchantment. But already, the year before, financial difficulties had forced the government to abolish the subsidy for building higher. By 1970 under 2 per cent of new local authority housing was in the form of flatted towers. High-rise housing had proved to be a brief departure from the traditions of British building, but it seriously damaged public confidence in planning and public housing, and it has left an indelible mark on our urban landscape.[28]

Past Landscapes

Landscape history is not just concerned with explaining the origins of today's landscapes. It is a source of historical information which can widen and deepen our understanding of earlier times, and of the nature and direction of historical change.

Up to a point, this was realized long before the systematic study of landscape history began in the 1950s. A century earlier Lord Macaulay had recognised the importance of trying to visualize past landscapes. 'If we would study with profit the history of our ancestors', he argued, 'we...must never forget that the country of which we read was a very different country from that in which we live.' The famous third chapter of his *History of England,* a 'description of the state' of the country in 1685, was the result.

> Could the England of 1685 be, by some magical process, set before our eyes, we should not know one landscape in a hundred or one building in ten thousand...Many thousands of square miles which are now rich corn lands and meadow, intersected by green hedgerows, and dotted with villages and pleasant country seats, would appear as moors overgrown with furze, or fens abandoned to wild ducks. We should see straggling huts built of wood and covered with thatch, where we now see manufacturing towns and seaports renowned to the farthest ends of the world. The capital itself would shrink to dimensions not much exceeding those of its present suburb on the south of the Thames.[29]

In our own century, several historians have sought to emulate Macaulay. Sir John Clapham produced two vivid studies of 'the face of the country' in the 'twenties and 'eighties of the nineteenth century, G.M. Trevelyan sketched a 'picture of England' as it was in the early eighteenth century, and J.D. Mackie and A.L. Rowse have portrayed England in the early and late sixteenth century respectively.[30]

Each of these accounts can excite our historical imagination, but they tend to treat the landscape as the background to their main concerns, political, social or economic history. Today, our increasing knowledge of past landscapes can contribute much more than an added sense of reality to the study of earlier times.

Landscapes and Societies

Landscapes reflect the societies that create them, their values and priorities, their social distinctions, and their stage of economic and social development. Discoveries about past landscapes can be of crucial importance for our understanding of periods when agriculture was the foundation of the economy and culture, and more conventional historical sources are not available.

Perhaps the biggest weakness of Professor Hoskins's pioneering book on the English landscape is the scant attention he paid to the prehistoric and even the Roman periods. Though he recognised the great age of some parts of the landscape, he assigned its real beginnings to the Saxon period when, he believed, the forests were cut down and the land turned over to agriculture.

Such views are no longer tenable today. Aerial photography, fieldwork, excavation, and paleobotanical studies have begun to reveal, for the first time, what the prehistoric landscape was really like. One result is that the time-scale of the creation of the English landscape has been greatly lengthened. It is now believed that the clearing of the natural wilderness, the 'wildscape' as Peter Fowler has called it, began as early as 5000 B.C. and that substantial parts of Britain were under cultivation by the middle of the fourth millennium B.C. By 1500 B.C. the division of the land into fields was widespread and there is even evidence of woodland management. The process of clearing the land was not continuous but marked by ebb and flow, often the result of changing climatic conditions or soil impoverishment. There was a major setback in the period 3000 to 2500 B.C., for example, when there are signs of over-population. After 2000 B.C., however, the climate became warmer and drier, and renewed advance was expressed in terms of more settlements and increasing evidence of cultivation.

Despite these fluctations, it now seems certain that most parts of England were exploited agriculturally in prehistoric times, not just the familiar chalk downlands, but also the heavy claylands and even the open heaths and moorlands of upland Britain once thought uninviting to early settlement. We have to visualise a landscape of enclosed fields, extensive pastures and a scatter of settlements and farmsteads (**Figure 5**). So Caesar did not exaggerate when he wrote of Kent that 'the population is exceedingly large...[and]...the ground thickly studded with homesteads'.[31]

The implications of these discoveries are considerable. Such a carefully exploited landscape means that we have underestimated the economic and technological achievements of prehistoric times. It also indicates the existence of a numerous and well-organised population. If the great enclosures, linear ditches and stone monuments lose in consequence something of their mystery, they have at last an intelligible setting.

Change and the Landscape

Landscapes alter with the societies which create them, and there can be few historical changes that are not reflected directly or indirectly in the man-made environment. Thus the religious revolution of the reign of Henry VIII left its mark on the landscape in the form of the most striking visible expression in Britain of a deliberate break with the past. The eight hundred and more monasteries founded in the Middle Ages had influenced the landscape in important ways. The Benedictines had played a crucial part in the reclaiming of the fens, and some Cistercian houses had depopulated whole areas to provide the solitude they desired. Yet other abbeys, notably in the north-east, had engaged in small-scale industrial activities and coal mining. Most important of all, throughout the country the great monastic buildings proclaimed the wealth and power of their communities. When Henry VIII's greed caused these religious houses to be dissolved with dramatic speed after 1536, one of the most influential institutions in the making of the landscape came to an abrupt end.

The most enduring legacy, the monastic buildings, suffered a varied fate. Fourteen great monastic churches survived the Dissolution, either because they were already

Figure 5: *Turnworth, Dorset: Iron Age fields and circular ditched farmstead.*

cathedrals, like Canterbury, or because they were transformed into cathedrals for new dioceses, like Peterborough. Upwards of a hundred other monastic churches continued in use for worship as parish churches. The bulk of monastic buildings, however, soon passed into lay hands as the confiscated estates were sold off. One effect was to stimulate building activity amongst the new owners. Lord Sandys, for instance, adapted the Augustinian priory of Mottisfont in Hampshire as a private mansion, adding brick wings. Other gentry owners, inhibited perhaps by feelings of uncertainty over their title and even fears of sacrilege, only began to build later in the century, and then often used the monasteries as sources of ready-worked building stone.[32] In the 1560s over 90 loads of stone from Waverley Abbey went to build Sir William More's new house at Loseley in Surrey, and the construction of the first Lord Fairfax's house at Nun Appleton in Yorkshire out of building stone from the nearby Cistercian nunnery prompted Andrew Marvell to write:

'And all that Neighbour-Ruine shows
The Quarries whence this dwelling rose.'[33]

As for the rest of the monastic buildings, John Freeman, one of Cromwell's deputies, indicated their intended fate when he wrote that 'the King's Commyssion commaundeth me to pull downe to the grownde all the walls of the Churches, stepulls, cloysters, fraterys, dorters, chapter housys, with all other howsys, savyny theym that be necessary for a farmer'.[34] But the task of 'plokyng down' the buildings proved too difficult and expensive, despite the use of gunpowder. The king had to be content with making them uninhabitable for conventual purposes by stripping the roofs and allowing the elements to do their worst.

The immediate effect was to convert into unsightly ruins what Robert Aske, one of the leaders of the Pilgrimage of Grace in 1536, had claimed were 'one of the beauties of this realm to all men and strangers passing through the same'.[35] Nearly twenty years after the Dissolution, the Venetian ambassador wrote of London that 'the city is much disfigured by the ruins of a multitude of churches and monasteries belonging heretofore to friars and nuns'.[36] In time the attitude to these crumbling edifices began to change as men were increasingly moved by their forlorn,

Figure 6: *Fountains Abbey, West Yorkshire. Fountains Hall, in the foreground, was built by Sir Stephen Proctor in the early seventeenth century mainly with stone from the monastic buildings. William Aislebie and his son John landscaped the area in the late eighteenth century.*

melancholy beauty, so redolent of the impermanence of human life and achievement. By the late seventeenth century, John Aubrey could write that 'the eie and mind is no lesse affected with these stately ruines than they would have been standing and entire. They breed in generous mindes a kind of pittie; and sett the thoughts a-worke to make out their magnificence as they were when in perfection'.[37] A century later, the Picturesque Movement brought a further shift in critical judgement; the three-dimensional landscape now came to. be judged by how far it would make a two-dimensional picture produced according to new canons of good taste. William Gilpin, the best known exponent of this new way of deriving aesthetic satisfaction from the land-scape, could even argue that these romantic, now ivy-clad, monastic ruins, were to be ranked amongst England's 'most picturesque beauties' whereas 'where popery prevails, the abbey is still intire and inhabited; and of course less adapted to landscape'.[38] Indeed, so prevalent was this appetite for ruinous beauty that the fifteen-year-old Jane Austen com-mented in her satirical *History of England* that the only thing to be said in favour of Henry VIII was that 'abolishing Religious Houses and leaving them to the ruinous depre-dations of time has been of infinite use to the landscape of England in general'.[39]

Though Gilpin was not above suggesting the judicious use of the mallet to improve the picturesque outline of Tintern Abbey, he strongly complained, when he visited Fountains Abbey, that by tidying up the ruins to make them a feature of a new landscape garden, the owner had 'pared away all the bold roughness and freedom of the scene and given every part a trim polish' (**Figure 6**).[40] Today, under the aegis of the Department of the Environment, tidying up is the universal policy.[41] Though this ensures the preservation of the ruins, some may share Gilpin's regret at the disappearance of so much of the nostalgic awe that once surrounded them.

Landscape as a palimpsest

Older landscape patterns, moreover, can crucially influence those that come later. Viewed from the air, the intricate pattern of rows of back-to-back houses in Leeds is bewilder-ing (**Figure 7**). What can account for these short, discon-nected streets, with their different alignments? The answer

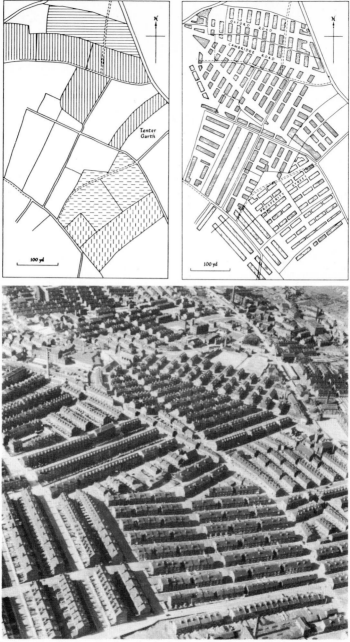

Figure 7: *Leeds: Back-to-back houses fitted into field and property boundaries. Fields to the south-west of Meanwood Road in 1847: four different owners are indicated by shading and the fifth is unshaded; (top left); The same area filled by back-to-back houses (top right); The same area from the air (bottom).*

lies in the way the city developed in the nineteenth century.

Leeds, the centre of the West Yorkshire woollen industry, experienced exceptional growth in those years; the population alone increased more than eight-fold to nearly 430,000 by 1901. This expansion was met by putting up back-to-back dwellings, described in 1908 as 'the characteristic feature of working-class housing' in the city. These were small houses built in double rows with each house joined to others at back and sides. Though present-day historians are divided whether the design derived from that of rural cottages or was first developed to fill the gardens behind older houses in the congested centre of the city, nineteenth-century social reformers were united in condemning back-to-backs for their restriction of light and the absence of through ventilation. Despite this, and the general prohibition of this type of housing in the Housing Act of 1909, they went on being built in the city until 1937, because they were easy and cheap to put up, and the low rents charged generally made possible occupation by a single family. Another reason was that this form of high-density housing was easily adapted to different field and plot sizes.

When the open fields around Leeds were enclosed in the later Middle Ages, they were divided amongst many small proprietors. There were no fewer than five different owners in the small area shown on the map in 1847 (**Figure 7**) Their field and property boundaries acted as the framework into which subsequent building activity was fitted. Speculative builders bought up fields as the owners were willing to sell, and arranged the streets and houses in them. This piecemeal development ensured, therefore, that field and property boundaries decisively influenced later housing patterns.[42]

Future Landscapes

Landscape history can serve a third purpose. By deepening awareness of our landscape heritage, it can play a crucial part in shaping our reactions to change in the present-day landscape, and in handling the vexed problem of conservation.

Past ages have been quite as destructive as our own. The general practice was for each generation to sweep away, uncomprehendingly, such of its predecessors' work which failed to conform to its own needs and aesthetic tastes. The Elizabethans, for example, were indifferent to medieval buildings and, as we have seen, often pillaged them for materials to construct their ostentatious new country houses.[43] By the eighteenth century the scale and pace of landscape change greatly increased. Hundreds of elaborate formal gardens were destroyed to satisfy the new taste of the English landscape movement, and the bare open landscape of the common fields was transformed into the geometrically shaped fields of parliamentary enclosure. Thousands of half-timbered houses were disguised with a veneer of fashionable Georgian brickwork, and it was rare for an owner to record a building, however important, before pulling it down.[44] Though the Victorians' treatment of country houses seems at times more restrained and conservative,[45] they destroyed as many as anyone, and covered up earlier work wherever possible. Churches suffered even more. By removing buildings and landscaping closes, James Wyatt and his Victorian successors enabled us better to appreciate medieval cathedrals by improving their settings. Yet all too often churches were vandalised in the act of 'restoring' them,[46] and 'one of the ironies of the Gothic Revival is that it largely destroyed the very buildings from which it drew its inspiration'.[47]

It is generally forgotten, moreover, that Victorians were utterly repelled by the Georgian environment. As Sir John

29

Summerson has reminded us, those Georgian streets and squares so highly regarded today, were denigrated for 'their meanness, poverty of scale, and lack of "character" '.[48] Whole areas of our towns and cities were demolished and redeveloped with scarcely a twinge of conscience. In London, much of the central area of the City, which dated from the rebuilding after the Great Fire, was swept away between 1857 and 1877.[49] In the 1870s central Bradford underwent an even more drastic redevelopment. Such was the scale and speed of the changes that the *Bradford Observer* commented that people who had been away for a few years did not recognise the town on their return:

> All was changed. Palatial warehouses, magnificent shops, imposing churches, large hotels, splendid public buildings, beautiful mansions and new streets without end arose out of the ruins, and Bradford with its new face of stone was something for the artistic mind to admire.[50]

Change was exhilarating, a sign of progress and of commercial success. It was embarked upon without much regard for what was being swept away. Few argued, like John Ruskin, that there is 'no question of expediency or feeling whether we shall preserve the buildings of past times or not. We have no right whatever to touch them. They are not ours'.[51] So it is salutary to remember that much of what survives of earlier landscapes has survived fortuitously. If the Victorians could have swept it away they would have. Just as certainly, if there had been a Tudor and Stuart, or Georgian preservation society in the nineteenth century, many notable buildings and landscapes would never have come into being.

In this century the pace and scale of landscape change has seemed greater than ever. Vast areas of our cities have been torn down to make way for shopping precincts and tower blocks. Every year 45,000 acres of agricultural land are swallowed up to meet the needs of industry, housing and roads, thousands of miles of hedges are uprooted to satisfy the demands of industrialised farming, and modern ploughing is obliterating ridge-and-furrow and the sites of deserted villages at an alarming rate. Little wonder the farmer is no longer 'seen as the nation's unpaid landscape gardener'.[52]

More depressing still, the greater our power to create new landscapes, the more we have lost confidence that our new landscapes are superior to those they replace. Preservation and amenity societies have multiplied in response to this feeling. To the Society for the Protection of Ancient Buildings and the National Trust, founded in 1877 and 1895 respectively, have been added, in this century, the Council for the Protection of Rural England (1926), the Georgian Group (1937), the Civic Trust (1957), the Victorian Society (1958), SAVE Britain's Heritage (1975), the Historic Landscapes Steering Group (1978), and a host of other bodies. As a result of the various Ancient Monuments Acts, beginning in 1882, some 20,000 monuments, mainly ruins and earthworks, are now protected. Yet the feeling persists that the essential character of the British landscape is still being destroyed.

How can the study of landscape history help us in coping with these problems? Can it enable us to establish the limits of both preservation and change? A few possibilities can be examined here.

The Fate of our Hedgerows

The history of threatened landscapes or landscape features is often a vital key to their importance. 'Without hedges', wrote Richard Jefferies in 1884, 'England would not be England.'[53] A century later, most people would share that view. Hedgerows are the most familiar and distinctive feature of our landscape; elsewhere in the world they are found only in Ireland, New England, Tasmania and parts of France. Different hedge types and layouts, moreover, are a key to the subtle regional character of our countryside. The straight eighteenth- and nineteenth-century hawthorn and ash hedges of the Midlands, for example, are quite unlike the older, meandering, thickly timbered hedgerows, known locally as 'shaws', of the Weald of Kent and Sussex.

Today, new agricultural systems and techniques, especially the spread of mechnization and the switch to arable farming facilitated by government subsidies, are threatening many hedgerows; at least a quarter (over 120,000 miles) have been grubbed out since the Second World War. The scale of these changes has produced an outcry.[54] Not only is the habitat of many animals and plants disappearing, but, the critics complain, the appealing variety of our countryside is giving place to dull monotony.[55]

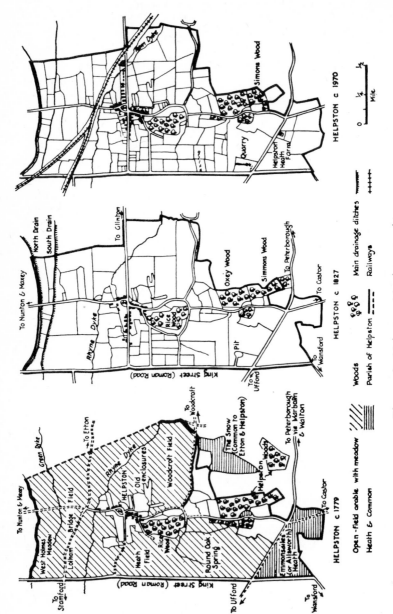

Figure 8: *Helpston, Northamptonshire.*

One useful contribution that the landscape historian can make is to put this controversy in historical context. To begin he must correct the commonly held view, expressed as recently as 1970 by Mr John Mackie, Joint Parliamentary Secretary to the Ministry of Agriculture, that 'all the hedges in our countryside have been man-made in the last two or three hundred years'.[56] In fact, many hedges can be traced back to Medieval times, and altogether between a third and a half of English hedgerows were planted before 1700. Over much of the Midlands, on the other hand, hedges are relative latecomers, the result of parliamentary enclosure in the eighteenth and nineteenth centuries. Though symbolic of the new England of agricultural improvement, the planting of these hedges was itself controversial. Early in the nineteenth century, Mary Russell Mitford, in her popular book *Our Village: Sketches of Rural Character and Scenery,* praised the beauty of the unenclosed landscape of her home village of Three Mile Cross, between Reading and Basingstoke. 'We have the good fortune', she wrote, 'to live in an unenclosed parish and many thank the wise obstinacy of two or three sturdy farmers, and the lucky unpopularity of a ranting madcap lord of the manor.'[57] When, in nearby Northampton-shire, the tide of enclosure eventually engulfed his native Helpston and the surrounding area, the poet John Clare, his sense of place offended by the alien pattern of fields imposed from outside, lamented:

> Fence now meets fence in owners little bounds
> Of field and meadow large as garden grounds
> In little parcels little minds to please
> With men and flocks imprisoned ill at ease...[58]

In some places, like Helpston, the original fields soon proved too large for grazing purposes and were in their turn, divided into smaller parcels (**Figure 8**). Elsewhere, hedgerows often began to be removed almost as soon as they were laid out. By the 1840s, a new wave of agricultural reformers was advocating hedge-grubbing to facilitate mechanised agricul-ture and let in air and light on animals and crops. By 1860, in Miss Mitford's adopted county of Berkshire, one advocate could assert that 'all practical men are pretty well agreed...that hedgerows are a great bar to agricultural improvement'.[59]

Figure 9: *Longleat, Wiltshire: Kip's engraving, c.1700, ornamental canal and gardens to the east of the house.*

Hedgerows, then, were not created as visual features or wildlife habitats; they fulfilled a need as stockproof barriers and as shelters. As agricultural and social needs have changed, so have the number and pattern of fields. The great peak of hedgerow removal, the 1960s, is already long past, and the rate of loss may fall further as the Countryside Commission (founded in 1968), through its New Agricultural Landscapes schemes, continues to explore ways of reconciling the new agricultural techniques and the traditional rural scene.[60] What the landscape historian must try to ensure is that the most interesting hedgerows historically, those on farm, estate and parish boundaries, which can tell us so much about the agricultural past of our country, are identified and not needlessly destroyed.

Changing Landscape Tastes

To study landscape history is soon to be made aware that landscape taste changes, and that the types of landscapes man has created solely to be admired have differed from period to period, mirroring changing aesthetic attitudes towards art and nature.[61] By alerting us to these vagaries of fashion, it can teach us humility and caution in our judgements on our own man-made environment and projected changes in it.

The English landscape garden is generally considered one of this country's greatest contributions to European art. It is typified by the serpentine lakes, meandering drives, and the vast expanses of rolling turf dotted with clumps of trees which are the settings of so many of our great country houses, and which seem amongst the most unaffected and unchanging features of our countryside. In fact, the natural look of these parks is highly misleading. They are the result of an eighteenth-century revolution in design in which landscape gardeners, of whom Lancelot (Capability) Brown (1715-83) is the most celebrated, rejected the excessively regimented formal gardens in vogue till then in favour of creating irregular, romantic surroundings for their patrons' country houses. To achieve the desired effects meant the manipulation of square miles of landscape, changing the courses of rivers, altering the profiles of hills, and planting trees on a vast scale. So when, in a poem by William Whitehead, Dame Nature protests that it was she who furnished 'the lawn, wood and water' which comprised the

Figure 10: Longleat, Wiltshire: Aerial photograph, taken in 1949, showing eighteenth-century landscaping of the park.

basic elements of the landscape garden, Brown could fairly retort:

> Who thinn'd, and who grouped, and who scattered those trees
> Who bade the slopes fall with that delicate ease,
> Who cast them in shade, and who placed them in light,
> Who bade them divide, and who bade them unite?
> The ridges are melted, the boundaries gone;
> Observe all these changes, and candidly own
> I have cloath'd you when naked, and when o'erdrest
> I have stripped you again to your bodice and vest.[62]

Not only are these parks carefully contrived works of art, but often enough they are not the settings orginally designed for the houses they surround. They were created by obliterating pre-existing gardens of very different types. Longleat in Wiltshire serves to illustrate this common, but largely unsuspected, historical discontinuity between house and surroundings. When Sir John Thynne built his gradiose Renaissance house, with its neat, symmetrical elevations, in the second half of the sixteenth century, it was probably surrounded by a typical Elizabethan garden made up of square and rectangular enclosures, each a different visual experience, bordered by walls or hedges. By the 1680s these had already given way to simple grassed enclosures when George London and Henry Wise laid out the vast asymetrical formal garden, with its axial walks and radiating alleys modelled on the fashionable French style, whose appearance is captured for us in Johannes Kip's magnificent engraving of about 1700 (**Figure 9**). It is melancholy to reflect that scarcely half a century later Lord Weymouth, responding to the dictates of a new fashion, and at a cost of £4,500, changed the layout so radically that a visitor remarked that 'the gardens are no more. They are suceeded by a fine lawn, a serpentine river, wooded hills, gravel paths meandering round a shrubbery, all modernised by the ingenious and much sought-after Mr Brown'.[63] It is this eighteenth-century park, modified in its turn by Humphry Repton in 1803, that we see today encircling a relatively unchanged sixteenth-century house, which is neverthless widely thought to accord with its surroundings (**Figure 10**). In realising the 'cap-abilities' of several hundred gardens, Brown and others

Figure 11: *The Colne Valley near Slaithwaite, West Yorkshire: pre-industrial revolution weavers' cottages overlook the Titanic Mill, built in 1912.*

obliterated a whole phase of visual creativity; an artistic movement lasting only half a century produced 'vandalism equal to anything that happens today, and all in the name of art'.[64]

Industrial Landscapes

Because it is concerned with the total man-made environment, landscape history also can help conservation groups avoid too narrow a preoccupation with conventionally beautiful landscapes. Most landscapes are not created, like landscape parks, simply to be admired; they are the bi-products of human activities such as farming, forestry and industry. As such, they are often ugly or have grim associations.

This is the case with the great textile mills of northern England, some of which survive little changed since they were built at the end of the last century and the beginning of this. With new economic conditions, many are now redundant, and others are under-used. Oldham, alone, has planned to demolish over 100 by the end of the century, leaving fewer than 20 in the town.

Such a clearance policy seems as insensitive and misguided as the wholesale destruction of so many magnificent formal gardens in the eighteenth century. Many of the mills are capable of being adapted to new business purposes or even housing. They represent, moreover, a building type peculiar to the area, and for that reason often undervalued elsewhere. More important still, in the Colne Valley, for instance, especially between Huddersfield and Marsden, where the austere, monumental mills, with their soaring chimneys, are still overlooked by the rough-hewn, millstone grit, pre-industrial revolution weavers' cottages on the hillsides above, we have a landscape which still vividly evokes some crucial stages in our industrial history (**Figure 11**). Carefully adapted and preserved, this whole district could continue to enrich the quality and variety of our landscape and be a source of endless historical fascination to future generations.[65]

The Inevitability of Change

Most important of all, the study of landscape history prepares us for the inevitability of change in the landscape of our own times. It brings to our notice what in the past has been needlessly destroyed or has disappeared through neglect. It may indicate those parts of the contemporary landscape which we should try to protect from violent and insensitive change. But for us to try to do more would be mistaken and, in any case, doomed to failure. The landscape has changed and it will always change; it cannot be fossilized or preserved as a museum piece.

If we cannot always welcome that fact, we may at least see its compensations. For it is time, not conscious planning, which has given our landscape its special diversity and fascination.

Notes and Select Bibliography

NOTES

1. I am grateful to Christopher Taylor and Philip Riden for reading and commenting on the draft of this essay.
2. T.D. Kendrick, *British Antiquity* (1950); M. Hunter, *John Aubrey and the Realm of Learning* (1975); D. Watkin, *The Rise of Architectural History* (1980).
3. For the development of Hoskins's views see D.W. Meinig, 'Reading the Landscape. An Appreciation of W.G. Hoskins and J.B. Jackson' in D.W. Meinig (ed), *The Interpretation of Ordinary Landscapes* (New York, 1979), pp. 195-244. J.B. Jackson is the pioneer of landscape history in the USA.
4. *The Making of the English Landscape* (1977 edition), p. 20.
5. O.G.S. Crawford, *Wessex from the Air* (Oxford, 1928); H.C. Darby (ed), *An Historical Geography of England before A.D. 1800* (Cambridge, 1936) cf. L. Dudley Stamp, *Man and the Land* (1st edition, 1955; 3rd edition, 1969).
6. *English Local History. The Past and the Future* (Leicester, 1966), p. 21.
7. *English Landscapes* (1973), and *One Man's England* (1978).
8. *One Man's England*, p. 69.
9. William Marshall in Nan Fairbrother, *New Lives, New Landscapes* (Pelican edition, 1972), pp. 11-12.
10. E.g. Hoskins's assertion in *English Landscapes*, p. 27, that Staverton Park, East Suffolk, is 'an untouched natural landscape', is corrected in O. Rackham, *Ancient Woodland: its History, Vegetation and Uses in England* (1980), pp. 293-4.
11. M. Morgan, *Historical Sources in Geography* (1979).
12. J.B. Harley, *Maps for the local historian. A guide to British sources* (1972); J.B. Harley and C.W. Phillips, *The Historian's Guide to Ordnance Survey Maps* (1964).
13. K. Cameron, *English Place-names* (3rd edition, 1977); Margaret Gelling, *Signposts to the Past. Place-names and the History of England* (1978); Margaret Faull, 'Place-names and Past Landscapes', *Eng. Place-Name Soc. J.*, xi (1978-79), pp. 24-46.
14. J. Harris, *The Artist and the Country House. A History of Country House and Garden View Painting in Britain 1540-1870* (1979)
15. M.D. Hooper, *Hedges and Local History* (1972), and 'Historical Ecology' in A. Rogers and T. Rowley (eds), *Landscapes and Documents* (1974), pp. 41-48.
16. W.G. Hoskins, 'Editor's Introduction', to H.P.R. Finberg, *The Gloucestershire Landscape* (1975 edition), p. 18.
17. A. Rogers and T. Rowley (eds), *Landscapes and Documents* (1974); T. Rowley and M. Aston, *Landscape Archaeology* (1974); C. Taylor, *Fieldwork in Medieval Archaeology* (1974).
18. Peirce F. Lewis, 'Axioms for Reading the Landscape' in D.W. Meinig (ed), *The Interpretation of Ordinary Landscapes* (New York, 1979), p. 12.
19. W.G. Hoskins, *Provincial England* (1963), p. 228.
20. J.M. Lambert et al., *The Making of the Broads* (Royal Geog. Soc. Res. Series, no. 3, 1960); M.W. Beresford and J.K.S. St Joseph (eds), *Medieval England. An Aerial Survey* (2nd edition, Cambridge, 1979), pp. 270-71.
21. C. Taylor, 'Polyfocal Settlement and the English Village', *Medieval Arch.*, 21 (1977), pp. 189-93; P.H. Sawyer (ed), *Medieval English Settlement* (1979); C. Taylor, 'Aspects of village mobility in medieval and later times' in Susan Limbrey and J.G. Evans (eds), *The Effect of Man on the Landscape: the Lowland Zone* (CBA Res. Rep. no 21, 1978), pp. 126-134; P. Bigmore, 'Villages and Towns' in L. Cantor (ed), *The English Medieval Landscape* (1982), pp. 154-74.
22. Beresford and St Joseph, op.cit., pp. 104-6.
23. W.G. Hoskins, 'The Rebuilding of Rural England, 1570-1640', *Past and Present* 4 (November, 1953), pp. 44-59; R. Machin, 'The Great Rebuilding: A Reassessment', ibid, 77 (November, 1977), pp. 33-56; E. Mercer, *English*

Vernacular Houses. A Study of Traditional Farmhouses and Cottages (1975).

24.   Hoskins, *Provincial England,* pp. 121-23.

25.   M.W. Beresford, *The Lost Villages of England* (4th imp. with corrections, 1963); M.W. Beresford and J.G. Hurst (eds), *Deserted Medieval Villages* (1971); R. Muir, *The Lost Villages of Britain* (1982).

26.   Urban housing in Scotland more closely resembles the flatted pattern of Continental Europe, see D. Niven, *The Development of Housing in Scotland* (1979).

27.   Cf. the famous pull-out drawing in his *Ghastly Good Taste: or, a depressing story of the rise and fall of English architecture* (1st edition, 1933; 2nd edition, 1970).

28.   P. Dunleavy, *The Politics of Mass Housing in Britain, 1945-1975* (Oxford, 1982), examines the processes which created the post-war flatted estates, with case studies of Birmingham, Bristol and the Inner London borough of Newham; see also A. Sutcliffe (ed), *Multi-Storey Living. The British Working Class Experience* (1974) and L. Esher, *A Broken Wave. The Rebuilding of England 1940-1980* (1981), especially the chapter on Sheffield, pp. 194-216. Suburbia is now being rehabilitated, see A.M. Edwards, *The Design of Suburbia: a critical study in environmental history* (1981), and P. Oliver, I. Davis and I. Bentley, *Dunroamin: the suburban semi and its enemies* (1981).

29   Lord Macaulay, *The History of England from the Accession of James the Second,* (ed) C.H. Firth, Vol I (1913), pp. 270, 272. For the chapter generally, see C.H. Firth, *A Commentary on Macaulay's History of England* (1938), chapter vi.

30.   J.H. Clapham, *An Economic History of Modern Britain,* Vol I (1926), Vol II (1932); G.M. Trevelyan, *England under Queen Anne,* Vol I (1930); J.D. Mackie, *The Earlier Tudors 1485-1558* (Oxford, 1952); A.L. Rowse, *The England of Elizabeth* (1950).

31.   R. Mercer (ed), *Farming Practice in British Prehistory* (Edinburgh, 1981); J.G. Evans, Susan Limbrey and H. Cleere (eds), *The Effect of Man on the Landscape: the Highland Zone* (CBA Res. Rep. no 11, 1975); Susan Limbrey and J.G. Evans (eds), *The Effect of Man on the Landscape: the Lowland Zone* (CBA Res. Rep. no 21, 1978).

32.   M. Airs, *The Making of the English Country House 1500-1640* (1975).

33.   H.M. Margoliouth (ed), *The Poems and Letters of Andrew Marvell,* Vol I (3rd edition, Oxford, 1971), pp. 65, 279-80.

34.   H. Ellis (ed), *Original Letters, Illustrative of English History* III, iii (1846), p. 268, cf. G.H. Cook (ed), *Letters to Cromwell and others on the Suppression of the Monasteries* (1965), p. 181.

35.   J. Gairdner (ed), *Letters and Papers, Foreign and Domestic, of the Reign of Henry VIII,* XII, part i (1890), pp. 405-6.

36.   R. Brown (ed), *Calendar of State Papers, Venetian,* V (1873), p. 543.

37.   Margaret Aston, 'English Ruins and English History: the dissolution and the sense of the past', *J. Warburg and Courtauld Inst.,* 36 (1973), p. 251.

38.   W. Gilpin, *Observations, Relative Chiefly to Picturesque Beauty...[on]...the Mountains, and Lakes of Cumberland, and Westmoreland,* Vol I (1792), p. 14.

39.   Jane Austen, *Love and Friendship, and other Early Works* (1922), p. 89.

40.   C. Hussey, *The Picturesque. Studies in a point of view* (1927), pp. 195-6.

41.   M.W. Thompson, *Ruins. Their Preservation and Display* (1981).

42.   M.W. Beresford, *Time and Place* (Leeds, 1961), pp. 5-9, and 'The Back-to-Back House in Leeds, 1787-1937' in S.D. Chapman (ed), *The History of Working-Class Housing: A Symposium* (Newton Abbot, 1971), pp. 93-132.

43.   J. Buxton, *Elizabethan Taste* (1963), chapter ii.

44.   An exception was Edward Conyers who had measured drawings and sketches prepared before the demolition of Copthall in Essex, see J. Newman, 'Copthall, Essex' in H. Colvin and J. Harris (eds), *The Country Seat: Studies in the History of the British Country House* (1970), pp. 18-29.

45.   M. Girouard, 'Living with the past: Victorian alterations to country houses' in

Jane Fawcett (ed), *The Future of the Past* (1976), pp. 117-139.

46.   G. Cobb, *English Cathedrals. The Forgotten Centuries: Restoration and Change from 1530 to the Present Day* (1980).

47.   Jane Fawcett, 'A Restoration tragedy: cathedrals in the eighteenth and nineteenth centuries' in Jane Fawcett (ed), *The Future of the Past* (1976), pp. 75-115.

48.   'London, the Artifact' in H.J. Dyos and M. Wolff (eds), *The Victorian City. Images and Realities,* Vol II (1973), p. 313.

49.   Ibid., pp. 312, 315.

50.   Vanessa Doe, 'Later Urban Landscapes' in A. Rogers and T. Rowley (eds), *Landscapes and Documents* (1974), p. 65.

51.   D. Lowenthal and H. Prince, 'English Landscape Tastes', *Geog. Rev.,* 55 (1965), pp. 205-6.

52.   Ibid., p. 200.

53.   Marion Shoard, *The Theft of the Countryside* (1980), p. 34.

54.   E. Pollard, M.D. Hooper and N.W. Moore, *Hedges* (1974); W.W. Baird and J.R. Tarrant, 'Vanishing Hedgerows', *Geog. Rev.,* 44 (1972), pp. 545-51.

55.   M. MacEwen, *Future Landscapes* (1976); R. Christian, *Vanishing Britain* (Newton Abbot, 1977); Marion Shoard, *The Theft of the Countryside* (1980).

56.   *Hansard,* Vol 797, col 1333.

57.   Vol I (1892 edition), p. 24.

58.   E. Robinson and G. Summerfield, *Selected Poems and Prose of John Clare* (1967), p. 170, see also J. Barrell, *The Idea of Landscape and the Sense of Place, 1730-1840* (Cambridge, 1972).

59.   J.B. Spearing, 'On the Agriculture of Berkshire', *J. Royal Agri. Soc.,* 21 (1860), p. 3.

60.   R. Westmacott and T. Worthington, *New Agricultural Landscapes* (1974).

61.   D. Lowenthal and H.C. Prince, *passim.*

62.   'The Late Improvements at Nuneham' in F. Emery, *The Oxfordshire Landscape* (1974), p. 130.

63.   Dorothy Stroud, *Capability Brown* (1975), pp. 85-6.

64.   M. Hadfield, *The English Landscape Garden* (1977), p. 8.

65.   M. Binney et al., *Satanic Mills* (1979); C. Aslet, 'Milltown Blues', *Country Life* (8 February 1979), pp. 336-37, cf. the work of the Ironbridge Gorge Museum Trust.

SELECT BIBLIOGRAPHY

London is the place of publication unless otherwise stated.

General Introductions
The best introduction to the development of the English landscape is still W.G. Hoskins, *The Making of the English Landscape* (new edition, 1977); for some of its limitations see C. Taylor, 'The Making of the English Landscape - 25 Years On', *The Local Historian,* 14 (1980-1), pp. 195-201. Popular accounts with different emphases are C. Trent, *The Changing Face of England* (1956); Penelope Lively, *The Presence of the Past. An Introduction to Landscape History* (1976); and E. Hyams, *The Changing Face of Britain* (1977). See also A.R.H. Baker and J.B. Harley (eds), *Man Made the Land* (Newton Abbot, 1973) and H.C. Darby (ed), *A New Historical Geography of England* (Cambridge, 1973).

For Wales, see F.V. Emery, *Wales* (1969); and Scotland, R.N. Millman, *The Making of the Scottish Landscape* (1975).

County and Regional Studies
K.J. Allison, *The East Riding of Yorkshire Landscape* (1976); J.H. Bettey, *The Landscape of Wessex* (Bradford-on-Avon, 1980); P. Bigmore, *The Bedfordshire and Huntingdonshire Landscape* (1979); P. Brandon, *The Sussex Landscape* (1974); F. Emery, *The Oxfordshire Landscape* (1974); H.P.R. Finberg, *The Gloucestershire Landscape* (1975); M. Havinden, *The Somerset Landscape* (1981); W.G. Hoskins,

Leicestershire (1957); R. Millward, Lancashire (1955); L.M. Munby, The Hertfordshire Landscape (1977); R. Newton, The Northumberland Landscape (1972); D.M. Palliser, The Staffordshire Landscape (1976); A. Raistrick, West Riding of Yorkshire (1970); M. Reed, The Buckinghamshire Landscape (1979); T. Rowley, The Shropshire Landscape (1972); N. Scarfe, The Suffolk Landscape (1972); J.M. Steane, The Northamptonshire Landscape (1974); C. Taylor, Dorset (1970); C. Taylor, The Cambridgeshire Landscape (1973); M. Williams, The South Wales Landscape (1975).

Rural Landscapes

R. Muir, Shell Guide to Reading the Landscape (1981), is lively and splendidly illustrated, and M.W. Beresford, History on the Ground. Six Studies in Maps and Landscapes (revised edition, 1971), conveys the excitement of landscape research.

The best introductions to the Medieval landscape are M.W. Beresford and J.K.S. St Joseph, Medieval England. An Aerial Survey (2nd edition, Cambridge, 1979), and L. Cantor (ed), The English Medieval Landscape (1982).

On fields and field patterns, see C. Taylor, Fields in the English Landscape (1975); E. Pollard, M.D. Hooper and N.W. Moore, Hedges (1974); and M.L. Parry and T.R. Slater (eds), The Making of the Scottish Countryside (1980). O Rackham, Trees and Woodland in the British Landscape (1976) is an important general study.

On villages, see T. Rowley, Villages in the Landscape (1978); R. Muir, The English Village (1980); and Gillian Darley, Villages of Vision (1975) – a study of villages created for aesthetic, philanthropic or political reasons.

Farmhouses and cottages are dealt with in N. Harvey, A History of Farm Buildings in England and Wales (1970); Gillian Darley, The National Trust Book of the Farm (1981); and M.W. Barley, The English Farmhouse and Cottage (1961).

On buildings generally, see J. and Jane Penoyre, Houses in the Landscape (1978); R.W. Brunskill, Traditional Buildings of Britain (1981); E. Mercer, English Vernacular Houses (1975); and P. Smith, Houses of the Welsh Countryside (1975). Important guides to the development of country houses are M. Airs, The Making of the English Country House 1500-1640 (1975) and M. Girouard, Life in the English Country House. A Social and Architectural History (1978).

For parks, see H. Prince, Parks in England (Pinhorns, Isle of Wight, 1967); L. Fleming and A. Gore, The English Garden (1979); M. Hadfield, The English Landscape Garden (Aylesbury, Bucks., 1977); C. Hussey, English Gardens and Landscapes, 1700-1750 (1967); and A.A. Tait, The Landscape Garden in Scotland 1735-1835 (Edinburgh, 1980).

For roads, see C. Taylor, Roads and Tracks of Britain (1979).

Urban Landscapes

The most useful general studies are M. Aston and J. Bond, The Landscape of Towns (1976); G.E. Cherry, Urban Change and Planning. A History of Urban Development in Britain since 1750 (1972); and I.H. Adams, The Making of Urban Scotland (1978). Particular aspects are covered in C.W. Chalklin, The Provincial Towns of Georgian England. A Study of the Building Process 1740-1820 (1974); W. Ashworth, The Genesis of Modern British Town Planning (1954); and H. Evans, New Towns: The British Experience (1972).

On buildings, see J. Burnett, A Social History of Housing 1815-1970 (1978); P.M. Eden, Small Houses in England 1520-1820 (Historical Association pamphlet, 1969); Vanessa Parker, The English House in the Nineteenth Century (Historical Association pamphlet, 1970); Enid Gauldie, Cruel Habitations. A History of Working-Class Housing 1780-1918 (1974); M.A. Simpson and T.H. Lloyd (eds), Middle Class Housing in Britain (Newton Abbot, 1977); S. Muthesius, The English Terraced House (1982); and J.B. Lowe, Welsh Industrial Workers Housing 1775-1875 (1977).

Amongst the many studies of particular towns and areas are H.J. Dyos, Victorian Suburb. A Study of the Growth of Camberwell (1966); D.J. Olsen, The Growth of Victorian London (1976); and M.J. Daunton, Coal Metropolis. Cardiff 1870-1914 (1977).

On industrial landscapes, see B. Trinder, The Making of the Industrial Landscape (1982); N. Cossons, The BP Book of Industrial Archaeology (1975); and B. Bracegirdle, The Archaeology of the Industrial Revolution (1973).

For railways, see M. Binney and D. Pearce (eds), Railway Architecture (1979).

CLIVE H. KNOWLES is
Senior Lecturer in History,
University College, Cardiff and
Chairman of the Society for
Landscape Studies founded in
1979. He is the author of an
earlier General Series pamphlet
on *Simon de Montfort, 1265-1965.*

Published by

THE HISTORICAL ASSOCIATION

[G107]